# Metaphor ReFantazio
# The Ultimate Guide

## Tod Shama

## Bav Kraft

## Disclaimer

The information presented in this guide is intended for educational and entertainment purposes only. While every effort has been made to ensure accuracy and comprehensiveness, game mechanics, features, and content are subject to change due to updates and patches from the developers of *Metaphor Refantazio*.

Players are encouraged to explore the game at their own pace and engage with the community for the latest strategies and tips. The experiences shared may vary based on individual playstyles, character builds, and updates to the game.

# Contents

# Introduction

## Overview of the Game

"Metaphor Refantazio" is not just another RPG; it's an evocative journey that intertwines deep storytelling with engaging gameplay mechanics, drawing players into a world where every choice and action resonates on multiple levels. Developed by a visionary team of storytellers and game designers, this title invites players to explore not only a fantastical realm but also the very essence of human experience through the lens of metaphor. Set against a backdrop of stunning visuals and a hauntingly beautiful soundtrack, the game captivates players from the moment they embark on their adventure.

At its core, "Metaphor Refantazio" challenges players to confront complex themes such as identity, perception, and transformation. Every character, quest, and environment is infused with symbolic meaning, encouraging players to delve deeper into the narrative. Players will find themselves navigating not only the physical world but also the intricate emotional landscapes that define the characters they meet. The developers have crafted a game that reflects the struggles, triumphs, and nuances of the human condition, making it a truly immersive experience.

Themes and Setting

The game is set in a sprawling, richly textured world that feels alive with history and culture. From bustling cities filled with vibrant characters to serene landscapes that evoke introspection, the environments are designed to encourage exploration and discovery. The realm itself is steeped in myth, with lore that invites players to piece together the stories of the land's past and its inhabitants. As players venture through various regions, they will encounter factions that embody different philosophies and worldviews, each adding layers of complexity to the overarching narrative.

Central to the game are the themes of self-discovery and the search for meaning. Players will face moral dilemmas and choices that challenge their understanding of right and wrong, often forcing them to reflect on their own values and beliefs. The metaphorical aspects of the game serve as both a narrative device and a gameplay mechanic, allowing players to interact with their environment and characters in unique ways. This approach not only enriches the storytelling but also enhances the player's emotional investment in the game.

Unique Features

One of the most striking features of "Metaphor Refantazio" is its innovative metaphor system, which allows players to harness symbolic representations of their experiences and emotions.

This system is intricately woven into the gameplay, providing players with the tools to solve puzzles, engage in combat, and navigate the story. Each metaphor is crafted to reflect not only the character's internal struggles but also broader societal issues, inviting players to think critically about their choices and the consequences that follow.

Additionally, the game boasts a dynamic narrative structure that adapts to player decisions, ensuring that no two playthroughs are alike. This feature encourages players to experiment with different approaches, discovering new facets of the story and its characters with each decision. Whether players choose to be diplomatic, confrontational, or strategic, the game responds in ways that feel organic and rewarding.

Furthermore, the character customization options are extensive, allowing players to create unique avatars that align with their playstyle and personal narrative. Skill trees are designed to offer meaningful choices, ensuring that each character can evolve in a way that reflects the player's journey and decisions.

In summary, "Metaphor Refantazio" is a game that dares to challenge conventional storytelling and gameplay mechanics, providing an ultimate experience that resonates on both emotional and intellectual levels. As players embark on this epic journey, they will find themselves not just as participants in a game, but as explorers of a rich tapestry of metaphor and meaning.

# Chapter One

# Gameplay Mechanics

Core Gameplay Loop

At the heart of "Metaphor Refantazio" lies a carefully crafted core gameplay loop that keeps players engaged and invested in their journey. The loop revolves around exploration, interaction, conflict, and growth, creating a rhythm that feels both satisfying and dynamic.

Exploration is the first phase, where players navigate a vast, beautifully rendered world filled with diverse environments. Each area is meticulously designed, with secrets waiting to be uncovered and unique characters to meet. The sense of discovery is palpable, encouraging players to roam freely, observe their surroundings, and immerse themselves in the rich lore embedded within the landscapes.

Interaction is seamlessly woven into the exploration phase. As players encounter NPCs, they can engage in meaningful dialogues that often present choices influencing the narrative. These interactions provide context, reveal character backstories, and deepen the player's connection to the world. Importantly, conversations often include metaphorical elements, reflecting the internal struggles of the characters and the larger themes of the game.

Conflict emerges as players encounter enemies and face challenges that test their skills. Combat is not merely about defeating foes; it's an opportunity to apply learned strategies, utilize acquired skills, and experiment with different approaches. The battles are designed to be exhilarating yet meaningful, with each encounter contributing to the player's sense of progression and mastery.

Finally, growth ties the loop together. Players earn experience through exploration, interaction, and combat, leading to character development and the unlocking of new abilities. This progression system feels rewarding and organic, providing players with a sense of accomplishment as they shape their characters and narrative paths.

Controls and Interface

"Metaphor Refantazio" features an intuitive control scheme designed to enhance the player's experience. Whether using a controller or keyboard and mouse, the controls are responsive, allowing players to navigate the environment fluidly. The layout prioritizes accessibility, ensuring that both newcomers and experienced gamers can quickly adapt.

The interface is minimalistic yet informative, designed to avoid overwhelming players while still providing essential information. The HUD displays vital stats, such as health and resources, without cluttering the screen, allowing players to remain focused on the action. Important prompts appear contextually, guiding players through interactions, combat, and exploration without breaking immersion.

Players can easily access their inventory and skill trees through well-organized menus, making it simple to manage items, gear, and abilities. The inventory system is thoughtfully designed, allowing players to categorize and search for items effortlessly. Crafting materials, equipment, and consumables are easily distinguishable, encouraging players to engage with the crafting mechanics without frustration.

Character Progression

Character progression in "Metaphor Refantazio" is a multifaceted system that rewards players for their engagement with the game world. As players complete quests, defeat enemies, and explore, they earn experience points that contribute to leveling up. Each level grants players skill points, which can be allocated to various abilities within a rich skill tree.

The skill trees are designed to cater to different playstyles, allowing players to tailor their characters to their preferences. Whether players prefer a direct combat approach, stealthy maneuvers, or powerful magic, the skill trees provide ample opportunities for customization. This depth of progression encourages experimentation, inviting players to try different builds and strategies.

Additionally, the game incorporates a unique metaphorical progression system. As players engage with the metaphor mechanics, they can unlock metaphor-specific abilities that enhance their gameplay experience. These abilities reflect the character's emotional and psychological journey, reinforcing the game's themes and allowing players to feel a deeper connection to their avatars.

Beyond numerical growth, character progression also involves narrative development. As players make choices throughout the game, the story adapts, leading to different character arcs and outcomes. This element of progression emphasizes the importance of player agency and the impact of decisions, ensuring that each playthrough feels distinct and meaningful.

Combat Mechanics

Combat in "Metaphor Refantazio" is a thrilling blend of action and strategy. The game utilizes a real-time combat system that rewards quick reflexes and tactical thinking. Players can execute a variety of attacks, ranging from basic strikes to complex combos, creating a fluid combat experience that feels dynamic and engaging.

Each character class offers unique abilities and combat styles, allowing players to find a fighting style that resonates with them. Players can switch between melee and ranged attacks, utilize special skills, and deploy metaphors that enhance their combat effectiveness. This versatility encourages players to adapt their strategies based on the enemies they face, promoting a sense of creativity in combat.

Enemies in "Metaphor Refantazio" are designed with distinct behaviors and weaknesses. Some may require players to use stealth and strategy, while others may demand all-out aggression. This diversity keeps combat fresh and exciting, as players must learn to read their opponents and adjust their tactics accordingly.

The game also features a robust boss battle system, where players face off against formidable foes that challenge their skills and understanding of the mechanics. Boss encounters often include multi-phase battles that require players to adapt their strategies on the fly, making these moments some of the most memorable in the game. Defeating a boss is not just about overcoming a challenge; it's a significant narrative milestone, often leading to profound character development and story progression.

Puzzle-Solving Elements

Puzzle-solving is a critical aspect of "Metaphor Refantazio," offering players an opportunity to engage their minds and creativity. Puzzles are thoughtfully integrated into the game world, often serving as gateways to new areas, lore, and character interactions. They range from simple environmental challenges to complex, multi-layered conundrums that require players to think critically and creatively.

The puzzles often incorporate the game's metaphor system, inviting players to interpret symbols and themes. For example, players might encounter a puzzle that requires them to align metaphors reflecting specific emotions or concepts, leading to a deeper understanding of the narrative and characters. This integration reinforces the game's themes and enhances the overall experience, making players feel as though they are actively participating in the story.

Environmental puzzles utilize the surroundings creatively. Players may need to manipulate objects, interact with elements in the environment, or combine abilities to unlock new pathways. These puzzles encourage exploration and experimentation, rewarding players who are observant and willing to think outside the box.

Some puzzles also incorporate a cooperative element, where players may need to work with NPCs or even other players in multiplayer modes to solve challenges. This aspect fosters a sense of community and teamwork, further enhancing the gameplay experience.

In summary, the gameplay mechanics of "Metaphor Refantazio" create a rich and immersive experience that encourages exploration, creativity, and meaningful interaction. With its engaging core loop, intuitive controls, deep character progression, dynamic combat, and innovative puzzles, the game invites players to lose themselves in a world of metaphor and meaning, ensuring that each moment is both rewarding and impactful.

# Chapter Two

## Story and Lore

The narrative of "Metaphor Refantazio" unfolds in a world brimming with depth and complexity, where each character's journey intertwines with larger existential themes. The story begins with a cataclysmic event that shatters the fabric of reality, creating rifts between various dimensions and causing metaphors to manifest as tangible entities. This disruption leads to chaos, as the inhabitants of the realm struggle to make sense of their altered lives and the new dangers that arise.

As players step into this world, they assume the role of a chosen protagonist who possesses the unique ability to navigate these metaphors. This ability allows them to interact with the very essence of the world, shaping their journey through choices that resonate on both personal and communal levels. The main plot revolves around the protagonist's quest to restore balance to the realms by confronting both the external threats posed by rogue metaphors and the internal conflicts that dwell within themselves and those they encounter.

The journey is not just about battling enemies; it's also a profound exploration of identity, purpose, and the intricacies of human emotion. The protagonist must gather allies, confront their past, and ultimately face a shadowy figure who represents the embodiment of despair, seeking to exploit the chaos for their own gain. The stakes escalate as the protagonist uncovers deeper truths about their abilities and the connection to the metaphors that shape their world.

Key Characters

The characters in "Metaphor Refantazio" are richly developed, each representing different facets of the human experience. The protagonist, whose name and gender can be customized by the player, serves as a vessel for exploring themes of self-discovery and growth. They are initially portrayed as uncertain and conflicted, but as the story progresses, their journey transforms them into a formidable force for change.

Supporting characters include a diverse cast, such as the wise mentor who guides the protagonist through their initial trials, a rebellious ally who embodies the spirit of resistance, and a tragic figure who has succumbed to despair. Each character has their own backstory and motivations, offering players multiple perspectives on the overarching conflict. Through interactions and dialogue choices, players can influence the relationships they build, leading to varied outcomes and character arcs.

Antagonists also play a crucial role in shaping the narrative. The primary antagonist, a mysterious figure known as the Shadow Weaver, is a master of manipulation and despair, representing the darker aspects of the human psyche. Their motivations are complex, driven by a desire to harness the metaphors for control rather than healing. This creates a compelling conflict, as the protagonist must confront not only external threats but also the internal struggles that the Shadow Weaver embodies.

Factions and Groups

The world of "Metaphor Refantazio" is populated by several factions and groups, each with its own beliefs and goals. These factions often embody different philosophies about the metaphors and their implications.

One notable faction is the Luminaries, a group of scholars and practitioners dedicated to understanding and harnessing the power of metaphors for the greater good. They seek to restore balance and heal the rifts created by the cataclysm. Their members often serve as mentors and guides for the protagonist, providing insight into the deeper meanings behind the metaphors and encouraging collaboration and unity.

In contrast, the Shadows represent a faction that thrives on chaos and despair. Comprised of those who have succumbed to their inner demons, this group seeks to exploit the metaphors for personal gain. Their motivations are steeped in a desire for power and control, making them formidable adversaries. As players navigate the world, they must confront not only the physical threats posed by the Shadows but also the philosophical dilemmas they present.

Another significant faction is the Wanderers, a nomadic group that believes in the fluidity of identity and the power of transformation. They view the metaphors as essential to understanding oneself and embrace the chaos as a means of growth. Their philosophy offers players an alternative perspective, encouraging exploration and self-discovery.

These factions often find themselves in conflict, with their beliefs clashing in dramatic ways. Players will engage with these groups through quests and interactions, and their choices can influence the power dynamics within the world, leading to different outcomes and alliances.

World-building Elements

The world of "Metaphor Refantazio" is meticulously crafted, with each region featuring its own distinct culture, geography, and history. From lush forests filled with ethereal creatures to desolate wastelands where despair manifests in tangible forms, the environments reflect the emotional landscapes of the characters that inhabit them.

Geographical landmarks often serve as metaphors themselves, symbolizing various emotional states or societal challenges. For instance, a towering mountain may represent the struggle for achievement and growth, while a dark, fog-laden valley might symbolize fear and uncertainty. As players traverse these landscapes, they not only engage with the environment but also reflect on the broader themes of the narrative.

The history of the world is rich with lore, recounting the rise and fall of civilizations that have grappled with the power of metaphors throughout the ages. Ancient texts and artifacts scattered throughout the land reveal the struggles of those who came before, providing players with context and depth as they uncover the mysteries of their surroundings. These lore elements enrich the storytelling, allowing players to piece together a tapestry of interconnected narratives that reflect the complexity of human emotions.

Additionally, the game's dynamic weather and day-night cycle contribute to the atmosphere and immersion. Changes in the environment often mirror the protagonist's emotional state or the narrative's progression, reinforcing the connection between character and world.

Mythology and Symbolism

Mythology and symbolism are woven into the very fabric of "Metaphor Refantazio." The game draws heavily from various cultural myths, reinterpreting them through the lens of personal struggle and transformation. The metaphors themselves are not just gameplay mechanics; they are representations of psychological and emotional states, allowing players to engage with profound concepts in an interactive manner.

Each metaphor encountered in the game carries its own narrative weight, often reflecting universal themes such as love, loss, fear, and hope. Players might encounter a metaphor representing "the weight of expectations" that manifests as a burdensome creature, forcing them to confront their own feelings of inadequacy. Engaging with these metaphors provides opportunities for character development and self-reflection, both for the protagonist and the player.

The symbolism extends beyond individual metaphors to encompass broader themes of interconnectedness and the cyclical nature of life. As players progress, they will encounter motifs that resonate with their own experiences, inviting them to explore their interpretations and meanings. This approach fosters a deeper emotional connection to the narrative, encouraging players to reflect on their own journeys as they navigate the complexities of the game.

In essence, "Metaphor Refantazio" is not just a game; it is a rich narrative experience that invites players to explore the depths of human emotion through a carefully constructed world filled with symbolism and lore. The story, characters, factions, and intricate world-building all combine to create a tapestry that is both profound and engaging, ensuring that players are not only entertained but also challenged to think critically about their own lives and the metaphors that shape their existence.

# Chapter Three

## Tips for New Players

Stepping into the world of "Metaphor Refantazio" can be both exhilarating and overwhelming. With its intricate mechanics and rich narrative, new players might find themselves navigating a landscape filled with choices, challenges, and opportunities for growth. To help ease this journey, here are some comprehensive tips designed to enhance your gameplay experience and ensure a smoother introduction to this fascinating realm.

Starting Strategies

As you begin your adventure in "Metaphor Refantazio," it's crucial to establish a solid foundation. Choosing your character class is one of the first and most significant decisions you will make. Each class comes with unique abilities and playstyles, so consider what resonates with you.

Whether you prefer to engage enemies head-on with a warrior class, employ stealth with a rogue, or wield powerful spells as a mage, make a choice that aligns with your preferences. This initial decision will shape your gameplay experience, influencing your approach to both combat and exploration.

Once you've settled on a class, take your time during the early stages of the game to familiarize yourself with the mechanics. Engage with NPCs, listen to their dialogues, and absorb the lore presented. Each conversation can provide valuable context and sometimes offer hints about upcoming challenges. Don't rush through initial quests; these often serve as tutorials that introduce essential gameplay mechanics and help you refine your combat skills.

Additionally, experiment with different strategies during encounters. Each enemy type has unique strengths and weaknesses, and understanding these will be key to your success. For instance, some enemies may be vulnerable to certain metaphors or abilities. By trying different approaches in combat, you'll quickly learn how to maximize your effectiveness.

Lastly, remember that "Metaphor Refantazio" encourages exploration. Don't hesitate to wander off the beaten path. Many hidden treasures, lore entries, and side quests are tucked away in less obvious locations, enriching your understanding of the world and providing valuable rewards.

Resource Management

Resource management is vital in "Metaphor Refantazio," where various items, skills, and metaphors play crucial roles in your survival and success. As you progress, you'll accumulate a range of resources, including health items, crafting materials, and currency. Learning how to manage these effectively can significantly impact your gameplay.

Start by paying close attention to your inventory. Organize your items to quickly access what you need during intense moments. It's easy to overlook crafting materials, but these resources can be essential for creating potions, gear, and other useful items. Make it a habit to regularly check your inventory and determine what you can craft or upgrade. This not only improves your overall capability but also encourages a deeper engagement with the game's mechanics.

Health management is another critical aspect. Keep a close eye on your health bar during battles and don't hesitate to use healing items when necessary. Remember that you can stockpile health items, so always be on the lookout for opportunities to gather or purchase these resources. Prioritize completing side quests and exploring environments where you can find hidden health items; these will be invaluable during tougher encounters.

Additionally, be mindful of the currency you collect. Spend it wisely on essential items rather than impulsive purchases. Investing in gear upgrades or powerful metaphors can have a more significant impact on your gameplay than acquiring cosmetic items. Look for vendors who offer unique items or crafting materials and weigh your options carefully.

Lastly, understand the importance of saving your game often. This practice is especially crucial before major encounters or decisions that could significantly alter your narrative path. Being able to revert to a previous save can save you from potential setbacks and allow you to explore different choices.

Navigating the World

Navigating the expansive world of "Metaphor Refantazio" requires both strategy and exploration. The game features diverse landscapes, each filled with its own challenges and secrets, so being adept at movement and orientation is essential.

Familiarize yourself with the map early on. The in-game map provides not only a layout of the areas you've discovered but also highlights quest markers and points of interest. Make it a habit to consult the map frequently, as it can guide you to your next objectives while helping you identify areas you haven't fully explored yet.

When exploring, take your time to engage with the environment. Many areas contain environmental puzzles that require observation and interaction. Look for clues that might indicate how to solve these puzzles or discover hidden pathways. Some areas may appear impassable at first glance but can be traversed with the right skills or abilities.

Pay attention to the dynamic weather and time of day within the game. These elements can influence enemy behavior and the availability of certain quests or items. For instance, some creatures may be more active during the night, while specific locations might change appearance based on the weather. Utilizing these environmental cues can enhance your exploration and improve your understanding of the world.

Additionally, engage with fast travel options as soon as they become available. Fast travel saves time and allows you to revisit previously explored areas quickly. However, always take a moment to consider what quests or collectibles you might have missed in each location before moving on. Revisiting places can often yield new interactions or rewards.

As you navigate through towns and villages, interact with the locals. Many NPCs offer quests, lore, or items that can aid your journey. Building relationships with these characters can also lead to interesting narrative developments and deeper immersion in the game's story.

Understanding the Metaphor System

One of the standout features of "Metaphor Refantazio" is its unique metaphor system, which serves as both a gameplay mechanic and a narrative device. Understanding this system is crucial for fully engaging with the game and enhancing your overall experience.

At its core, the metaphor system allows players to embody different aspects of emotion and thought, manifesting them as tangible abilities in the game. As you progress, you will unlock various metaphors that can be used in combat, puzzle-solving, and dialogue interactions. Each metaphor carries distinct effects, and knowing when to utilize them can turn the tide in both battles and story progression.

Begin by experimenting with the different metaphors you unlock. Each one has its own flavor and tactical advantage, whether it's boosting your damage, providing defensive capabilities, or influencing NPC interactions. The key is to understand the context in which each metaphor shines. For example, some metaphors may be particularly effective against specific enemy types, while others can enhance your abilities during certain quest scenarios.

Moreover, the metaphor system intertwines with the narrative. As you encounter characters and situations that resonate with specific emotions, the relevant metaphor can offer unique dialogue options and outcomes. This aspect encourages players to think critically about their choices and the themes at play in the story. Engaging with the metaphor system in this way adds layers of depth to your interactions and can lead to dramatically different outcomes based on the metaphors you choose to employ.

Additionally, consider how the metaphors relate to your character's development. As you navigate the world and confront various challenges, reflect on the emotional journeys of both your character and those they encounter. The game often prompts players to reconsider their understanding of themselves and others through the lens of these metaphors, enriching the overall narrative experience.

Finally, don't hesitate to revisit earlier areas with your newly acquired metaphors. This practice can reveal new pathways or dialogue options that weren't available before, offering deeper insights into the lore and enhancing your understanding of the characters.

By embracing these tips—focusing on your starting strategies, managing resources effectively, navigating the world with intention, and understanding the metaphor system—you'll set yourself up for success in "Metaphor Refantazio." This approach not only enhances gameplay but also enriches your emotional engagement with the narrative, ensuring a memorable and impactful journey.

# Chapter Four

## Character Builds

In "Metaphor Refantazio," character builds play a vital role in shaping the gameplay experience. The game offers a rich variety of classes and skill trees, allowing players to tailor their characters to fit their preferred playstyles. This depth of customization not only enhances combat effectiveness but also encourages players to immerse themselves in the narrative and themes of the game.

Class Overview

The classes in "Metaphor Refantazio" are designed to reflect different aspects of human experience and emotional states, each embodying unique abilities and traits. This thematic alignment with the game's narrative enriches the gameplay, as players can choose a class that resonates with their personal connection to the story.

The Warrior class is a stalwart choice for players who prefer a straightforward approach to combat. Warriors excel in melee combat, wielding heavy weapons and donning sturdy armor. Their abilities focus on dealing high damage while maintaining durability, making them ideal for players who enjoy engaging enemies head-on.

The Rogue class, in contrast, appeals to those who favor stealth and agility. Rogues are masters of evasion, able to navigate the shadows and strike swiftly. Their skills include high mobility and critical damage, allowing them to exploit enemy weaknesses effectively. This class is perfect for players who relish tactical combat and prefer to outmaneuver their foes.

Mages, on the other hand, harness the power of the elements and metaphysical energies. With a focus on spellcasting, Mages can deal massive area damage or support their allies with healing spells. Their versatility makes them a valuable addition to any party, and players who enjoy a more strategic approach will find the Mage class particularly rewarding.

Lastly, the Guardian class combines elements of both offense and defense. Guardians are equipped to protect their allies while dishing out significant damage. Their abilities often involve shielding teammates or drawing enemy fire, making them essential in cooperative play. Players who thrive in team-oriented environments may find the Guardian class to be a perfect fit.

Skill Trees and Customization

Each class in "Metaphor Refantazio" comes with a unique skill tree that allows for extensive customization. These skill trees are divided into different branches, each focusing on specific aspects of gameplay, such as combat abilities, support skills, or metaphor enhancements. As players gain experience and level up, they can invest skill points into these branches, unlocking new abilities and enhancing their character's strengths.

The skill trees are designed to encourage experimentation. For instance, a Warrior may choose to specialize in a heavy-hitting melee branch, focusing on devastating attacks, or opt for a more balanced approach by investing in defensive skills that bolster survivability. This flexibility allows players to create builds that align with their individual playstyles.

Rogues benefit from a variety of stealth and agility-related skills, enabling players to customize their approach to combat. Some may prioritize skills that enhance evasion and critical hit chances, while others might focus on traps and crowd control to manipulate the battlefield. This branching design allows for nuanced character development, encouraging players to adapt their strategies as they progress.

Mages have the option to specialize in elemental magic, healing, or support skills. Players can choose to wield powerful spells that deal damage over time or invest in abilities that provide utility to the team. This versatility encourages players to think strategically about their role in both combat and exploration.

Guardians offer a unique opportunity for hybrid builds. Players can invest in defensive skills that improve protection for allies or focus on offensive capabilities to become formidable frontline fighters. This flexibility allows players to adapt their role based on the party's composition and the challenges they face.

Customization goes beyond just skill points. Players can also choose gear, weapons, and items that complement their builds. Equipping specific armor sets or weapons can provide unique bonuses, further enhancing the effectiveness of a particular playstyle. The game encourages players to experiment with different combinations, promoting creativity and personal expression in character development.

Recommended Builds for Different Playstyles

Creating effective character builds in "Metaphor Refantazio" can greatly enhance your gameplay experience. Here are some recommended builds tailored to various playstyles, allowing players to maximize their potential based on their preferences.

For players who enjoy a straightforward combat experience, the **Berserker Warrior Build** is a fantastic choice. This build focuses on high damage output through aggressive melee attacks. Key skills to invest in include "Crushing Blow," which deals massive damage with a chance to stagger enemies, and "Unyielding Fury," which boosts attack power when health is low. Equip heavy armor for durability, and consider weapons with high critical hit rates to capitalize on this build's strengths.

The **Shadowblade Rogue Build** caters to players who prefer stealth and precision. This build emphasizes agility and critical damage, allowing players to dispatch foes quietly and efficiently. Skills like "Silent Steps," which enhances movement speed while crouching, and "Backstab," which increases damage dealt to unaware enemies, are essential. This build thrives on hit-and-run tactics, so equip lightweight armor for mobility and weapons that increase critical hit damage.

For those who appreciate a strategic approach to combat, the **Elementalist Mage Build** offers a balance of offensive and crowd control capabilities. Invest in skills like "Frost Nova," which immobilizes enemies in an area, and "Firestorm," which deals damage over time. This build excels at controlling the battlefield and providing support to allies. Equip gear that enhances spellcasting speed and boosts elemental damage to maximize effectiveness.

Players who thrive in cooperative environments may find the **Guardian Defender Build** to be the most rewarding. This build focuses on supporting teammates while maintaining a strong presence on the battlefield. Skills such as "Shield Wall," which absorbs damage for allies, and "Taunt," which draws enemy attention, are key. Equip heavy armor for resilience, and select weapons that deal moderate damage while offering utility, such as shields that provide bonuses to team defense.

For those who enjoy a mix of offense and support, the **Battle Mage Build** combines elements of both melee and magic. This hybrid build allows players to wield weapons while casting spells, making them adaptable in various situations. Skills like "Spellblade," which allows melee attacks to deal magical damage, and "Arcane Shield," which absorbs damage while increasing spell power, create a unique playstyle. Equip gear that boosts both physical and magical stats for optimal performance.

Finally, for players who enjoy a more versatile approach, the **Hybrid Guardian Build** combines offensive and defensive abilities. This build allows players to switch between dealing damage and protecting allies as needed. Invest in skills from both the Guardian and Warrior trees, such as "Guardian's Fury," which boosts damage dealt while defending, and "Protective Aura," which enhances teammates' defense. Equip a mix of armor that balances resilience and damage output to adapt to different scenarios.

In summary, character builds in "Metaphor Refantazio" offer players the opportunity to craft unique identities that resonate with their playstyles and preferences. With a variety of classes, skill trees, and customization options, players can experiment and adapt their characters to suit the challenges they face. Whether you choose to be a ferocious Berserker, a stealthy Shadowblade, a strategic Elementalist, a supportive Guardian, or a hybrid Battle Mage, the game invites you to explore the depths of character development while engaging in a rich narrative experience.

# Chapter Five

## Quests and Side Activities

In "Metaphor Refantazio," quests and side activities are fundamental to the overall experience, immersing players in a rich narrative while offering opportunities for character development, exploration, and engagement with the game's intricate world. The balance between main quests and side activities allows players to dive deeply into the story or take a more leisurely path, shaping their journey based on personal preferences.

Main Quests Overview

The main quests in "Metaphor Refantazio" form the backbone of the narrative, guiding players through the unfolding story and introducing key characters, locations, and thematic elements. These quests typically revolve around the central conflict of restoring balance to a world disrupted by metaphors, inviting players to engage with profound existential themes.

Each main quest is designed to challenge players not only in terms of combat but also through emotional and moral dilemmas. As players progress, they encounter pivotal moments that force them to make difficult decisions, shaping their character's journey and the world around them. The choices made during these quests can have far-reaching consequences, influencing future interactions and plot developments.

Main quests often culminate in dramatic encounters with significant antagonists, requiring players to utilize all the skills, metaphors, and strategies they've honed throughout the game. These encounters are not just about defeating enemies; they also serve as climactic moments that challenge players' understanding of their character's motivations and the larger implications of their actions.

Moreover, the narrative depth of the main quests is complemented by beautifully crafted cutscenes and dialogues, enhancing immersion and emotional engagement. The interplay between gameplay and storytelling ensures that players remain invested in the unfolding drama, prompting them to ponder the larger themes at play long after they've completed the quests.

Side Quests and Their Importance

Side quests in "Metaphor Refantazio" are just as crucial as the main narrative. While they may not drive the overarching plot, these quests enrich the gameplay experience by offering deeper insights into the world, its inhabitants, and the various metaphors that permeate the story. Engaging in side quests allows players to explore aspects of the game that may not be covered in the main storyline, revealing hidden lore and character backstories.

Many side quests involve unique challenges or puzzles that encourage exploration and critical thinking. For instance, players may be tasked with retrieving a lost item for a villager, which could lead them to discover a hidden area filled with lore-related collectibles. These quests often unveil local legends and stories, providing context that enhances the world-building and makes the player feel more connected to the environment.

Side quests also present opportunities for character development. Players can form bonds with NPCs through these interactions, influencing relationships and even unlocking special abilities or rewards. The emotional weight of these quests often resonates with players, prompting them to reflect on their choices and the consequences of their actions.

In addition, completing side quests can yield valuable resources, experience points, and unique items that are essential for character progression. The rewards gained from these activities can significantly enhance the player's ability to tackle main quests and challenges, making them an integral part of the overall gameplay loop.

Mini-Games and Challenges

"Metaphor Refantazio" features a variety of mini-games and challenges that offer a refreshing break from the main questline while providing unique rewards and experiences. These activities are not just filler; they are thoughtfully designed to complement the themes of the game and engage players in different ways.

Mini-games often revolve around skill-based tasks that test players' reflexes, strategy, or puzzle-solving abilities. For example, players may encounter a rhythm-based game where they must synchronize their actions with the music of the world, resonating with the game's emphasis on harmony and balance. Successfully completing these challenges can yield unique items or metaphor enhancements, rewarding players for their participation.

Another popular mini-game involves crafting, where players can gather resources and combine them in creative ways to produce powerful items or upgrades. This activity emphasizes resource management and encourages players to engage with the game's gathering mechanics while offering a satisfying sense of accomplishment.

Challenges also come in the form of timed trials or combat arenas, where players can test their skills against waves of enemies or compete for high scores. These challenges often feature leaderboards, adding a competitive element that encourages players to improve their performance and engage with the community.

Participating in these mini-games and challenges not only enhances the overall experience but also allows players to explore the world in a more lighthearted and enjoyable manner. They provide a welcome diversion from the often heavy themes of the main quests, creating a well-rounded gameplay experience.

Collectibles and Achievements

Collectibles and achievements play a vital role in "Metaphor Refantazio," rewarding exploration and dedication while adding layers of depth to the gameplay. Throughout the game, players can discover various collectibles, each contributing to the overarching narrative and world-building.

Collectibles often include lore entries, unique items, and metaphor fragments that can enhance the player's abilities or unlock new story elements. Finding these collectibles encourages thorough exploration of the game's expansive environments, as many are hidden in hard-to-reach locations or tied to specific side quests. The thrill of uncovering these items adds an element of discovery, compelling players to immerse themselves in every corner of the world.

Lore entries, in particular, enrich the game's narrative, providing context and background to the various factions, characters, and events that shape the story. Players who take the time to collect these entries will gain a deeper understanding of the game's themes and motivations, enhancing their overall engagement with the narrative.

Achievements serve as a form of recognition for players' accomplishments within the game. These can range from completing specific quests to mastering mini-games or discovering all collectibles. Achievements often come with unique rewards, such as cosmetic items, special titles, or even new gameplay mechanics. They encourage players to challenge themselves and explore aspects of the game they may not have considered, fostering a sense of completion and mastery.

Additionally, the achievement system often ties into the game's metaphor system, rewarding players for experimenting with different metaphors or approaches to combat. This aspect further reinforces the game's core themes of identity and transformation, allowing players to reflect on their growth as they progress.

In conclusion, quests and side activities in "Metaphor Refantazio" offer a rich and immersive gameplay experience. The intricate design of main quests and their emotional depth ensure that players remain engaged with the narrative, while side quests and mini-games provide essential opportunities for exploration and character development. Collectibles and achievements add layers of richness, rewarding players for their curiosity and dedication. Together, these elements create a well-rounded experience that encourages players to delve into the world and its myriad stories, making their journey not only about completion but also about discovery and personal growth.

# Chapter Six

# Exploration

Exploration in "Metaphor Refantazio" is a vital component that enriches the overall experience, inviting players to engage deeply with the world and its intricate lore. The game's meticulously crafted environments are not only visually stunning but also teeming with secrets, hidden treasures, and opportunities for interaction. Through exploration, players can uncover the layers of narrative that underpin the game, enhancing their connection to the story and its characters.

Key Locations

The world of "Metaphor Refantazio" is vast and diverse, featuring a myriad of key locations that serve as backdrops for the unfolding narrative. Each area is carefully designed to reflect the themes and emotional states that the game embodies, creating an immersive experience that captivates players.

One of the central hubs is **Elysium Town**, a vibrant settlement where players can interact with NPCs, accept quests, and access various services. The town serves as a social center, bustling with life and filled with hidden gems, such as cozy shops and intimate cafés. It's in Elysium Town that players can engage with the local community, learning more about the world's lore and the conflicts that drive the narrative forward.

Venturing beyond the town, players may discover the **Whispering Woods**, a lush forest filled with ancient trees and mystical creatures. The woods are shrouded in a sense of mystery, with winding paths that lead to breathtaking views and hidden glades. Exploring this area reveals side quests tied to the forest's guardians, whose stories are woven into the larger tapestry of the game's narrative.

The Whispering Woods not only serve as a stunning location for exploration but also as a reminder of the natural world's connection to the metaphors at play.

Another significant location is the **Ruins of Eldoria**, remnants of a long-lost civilization. This area is rich in history and lore, with crumbling structures and faded murals that hint at the stories of the past. Players can delve into the ruins to uncover artifacts that provide insights into the game's mythology, unlocking new quests and enhancing their understanding of the world. The sense of discovery in Eldoria is palpable, inviting players to piece together the fragments of history scattered throughout.

Secrets and Hidden Areas

One of the most rewarding aspects of exploration in "Metaphor Refantazio" is the plethora of secrets and hidden areas waiting to be discovered. These concealed gems not only enhance gameplay but also deepen the narrative, encouraging players to engage thoroughly with their surroundings.

Hidden areas often require players to solve environmental puzzles or utilize specific abilities to access them. For instance, players may encounter a seemingly insurmountable cliff face that can be scaled by using a specific metaphor or skill. Once at the top, they might find a secluded cave filled with valuable collectibles or lore entries that expand upon the game's rich history. These hidden areas serve as a testament to the developers' attention to detail, rewarding curious players who take the time to explore.

In addition to traditional hidden areas, players can stumble upon secret quests triggered by specific interactions with the environment or NPCs. For example, helping a lost traveler in a remote location might lead to a chain of events that unlocks a questline involving ancient guardians.

These quests often yield unique rewards and provide additional layers of depth to the narrative, making exploration feel purposeful and engaging.

Another layer of secrecy lies in the game's collectible items, often hidden in obscure locations that require thorough investigation. Players may find scrolls, artifacts, or unique metaphor fragments that not only enhance their character but also unveil fascinating lore. The thrill of uncovering these secrets can significantly enhance the sense of accomplishment and connection to the game's world.

Environmental Interactions

Environmental interactions are a cornerstone of exploration in "Metaphor Refantazio," adding a dynamic element that encourages players to engage with their surroundings. The game is designed to be interactive, with various elements in the environment responding to the player's actions and choices.

Players can manipulate objects in the world to solve puzzles or unlock new pathways. For instance, pushing a boulder to clear a blocked path or activating ancient mechanisms can lead to hidden chambers filled with treasure or lore. These interactions foster a sense of agency, allowing players to shape their journey through active engagement rather than passive observation.

The environment also reacts to players' choices, creating a living world that feels responsive and alive. Weather conditions, time of day, and even the emotional state of the character can influence gameplay. For instance, certain paths may be more accessible during specific weather conditions, or particular NPCs may only appear at night, adding layers of complexity to exploration.

Additionally, players can utilize metaphors in unique ways to interact with the environment. For example, a metaphor tied to nature may allow players to manipulate plants, causing them to grow or change form to reveal hidden pathways. These interactions not only deepen the gameplay mechanics but also align with the game's themes, emphasizing the interconnectedness of all elements within the world.

As players explore, they'll also encounter dynamic wildlife and NPCs that inhabit the environment. Engaging with these characters can lead to spontaneous side quests, trade opportunities, or even battles, enhancing the immersive experience. The diversity of interactions available encourages players to approach exploration with curiosity and creativity, ensuring that no two journeys are alike.

In conclusion, exploration in "Metaphor Refantazio" is an intricate and rewarding aspect of the gameplay experience. With key locations that invite players to delve into rich narratives, secrets that enhance the sense of discovery, and environmental interactions that create a dynamic world, players are encouraged to engage deeply with the game. The exploration aspect not only enriches the overall experience but also reinforces the game's themes of identity, connection, and transformation, making every moment spent in the world a meaningful part of the journey.

# Chapter Seven

# Combat Strategies

Combat in "Metaphor Refantazio" is a dynamic and integral part of the gameplay experience. Understanding the nuances of combat, from recognizing enemy types to optimizing team dynamics, is crucial for overcoming the challenges that lie ahead. Mastering these strategies not only enhances effectiveness in battle but also deepens the overall engagement with the game's themes and mechanics.

Enemy Types and Weaknesses

The game features a diverse array of enemy types, each with its unique abilities, strengths, and weaknesses. Familiarizing yourself with these can significantly impact your combat effectiveness.

**Melee Fighters** are the frontline brutes, often equipped with heavy weapons and high durability.

They rely on brute strength and tend to have moderate speed. The best strategy against these enemies is to use ranged attacks or mobility-based abilities to keep them at bay. Utilizing skills that exploit their slower movement can also be advantageous, allowing players to strike when they are vulnerable.

**Ranged Enemies** present a different challenge. They often attack from a distance, using arrows or magic to chip away at your health. The key to defeating these foes lies in closing the gap quickly or employing crowd control abilities to disrupt their attacks. Using terrain to your advantage—such as taking cover behind obstacles—can help mitigate damage while you plan your counterattack.

**Magic Users** are perhaps the most unpredictable enemies, utilizing powerful spells that can inflict status effects or area damage. To counter these foes, players should prioritize interrupting their casting by using abilities designed to stun or silence. It's also essential to keep moving to avoid being caught in damaging spells. Understanding the specific elemental affinities of magic users can also provide insight into their weaknesses; for instance, using fire-based attacks against ice-oriented mages can yield significant advantages.

**Summoners** are another unique enemy type, capable of calling forth additional foes to overwhelm players. Dealing with summoners requires a strategic approach; targeting them first can prevent their reinforcements from overwhelming the party. Skills that provide area damage or crowd control can effectively manage the additional threats while allowing players to focus on the summoner.

Boss Fights Tips

Boss fights in "Metaphor Refantazio" are designed to test players' mastery of combat mechanics, requiring not just skill but also strategy and adaptability. Each boss encounter typically features distinct phases and mechanics, necessitating careful observation and quick thinking.

Before engaging a boss, it's crucial to prepare adequately. Ensure that your character is fully equipped with appropriate gear, consumables, and abilities tailored to the specific boss you are facing. Understanding the boss's lore and mechanics can provide hints about their weaknesses and attack patterns.

During the fight, pay close attention to the boss's attack animations. Most bosses will telegraph their moves, providing windows for evasion or counterattacks. For example, if a boss raises its weapon or begins to glow ominously, it may indicate a powerful attack is coming. Recognizing these signals allows players to dodge or reposition effectively.

Utilizing the environment can also turn the tide in boss fights. Many arenas contain interactive elements or obstacles that can be used to your advantage. For instance, luring a boss into a trap or using pillars for cover can create opportunities for dealing damage while minimizing risk.

In multi-phase boss fights, each phase often introduces new mechanics or attack patterns. Be prepared to adapt your strategy as the battle evolves. This may involve changing your role—switching from a damage dealer to a support role if your allies are struggling—or focusing on avoiding damage during particularly intense phases.

Finally, teamwork is essential in boss encounters. Communicate with your team to coordinate attacks, share buffs, and provide support when needed. Combining abilities effectively can amplify damage and control, creating openings that can lead to victory.

Effective Use of Abilities

Abilities are the heart of combat in "Metaphor Refantazio," and understanding how to use them effectively can drastically improve your chances in battle. Each character class comes equipped with a unique set of abilities that can be combined to create devastating effects.

It's important to prioritize abilities that complement your playstyle and the composition of your team. For example, if you're playing as a Mage, consider focusing on crowd control spells that can immobilize enemies, allowing your teammates to unleash their attacks without fear of retaliation. If you're a Warrior, prioritizing skills that enhance your durability can allow you to take more risks on the frontline.

Timing is key when using abilities. Certain skills may have cooldowns or require specific conditions to be met. For instance, a powerful burst damage ability might be best saved for when a boss is vulnerable, while support abilities should be used strategically to ensure allies are kept alive during critical moments. Awareness of your team's status—health levels, resource availability, and positioning—can inform when to unleash your abilities for maximum impact.

The synergy between abilities is also crucial. Combining abilities from different classes can lead to powerful combos. For instance, a Mage's area-of-effect spell can be followed up by a Warrior's ability that amplifies damage against immobilized enemies. Identifying these opportunities can turn the tide of battle and lead to overwhelming enemy forces.

Additionally, some abilities may have secondary effects that can be exploited. For example, certain skills might apply debuffs to enemies, reducing their damage or resistance. Recognizing these interactions allows players to strategize effectively, focusing on weakening foes before dealing heavy damage.

Team Composition and Synergy

The composition of your team plays a vital role in the success of combat encounters in "Metaphor Refantazio." A well-balanced team can enhance effectiveness, allowing players to tackle challenges with a greater chance of success. Understanding the strengths and weaknesses of each class is essential for forming an effective party.

A balanced team typically includes a mix of damage dealers, tanks, and support characters. Damage dealers, such as Rogues and Mages, excel in dealing high amounts of damage but are often less durable. Tanks, like Guardians and Warriors, absorb damage and protect their teammates, allowing squishier classes to thrive. Support characters can heal, buff, or provide crowd control, ensuring the team maintains resilience during tough encounters.

Synergy between team members is crucial. Players should communicate about their abilities and strategies, coordinating attacks to maximize damage and control. For instance, if a Warrior is about to initiate an attack, the Mage can prepare a spell to follow up, creating a powerful combo that overwhelms enemies.

It's also important to adapt team strategies based on the enemy types encountered. If facing a group of melee fighters, positioning your tank at the forefront while allowing ranged characters to attack from a distance can create a strong frontline. Conversely, when dealing with magic users, it may be wise for damage dealers to focus on interrupting their casting while support characters maintain the team's health and status.

Lastly, players should be aware of the strengths and weaknesses of their chosen characters in relation to one another. If one character excels at dealing damage but lacks defensive capabilities, it's essential for teammates to cover that weakness. This might involve assigning roles during battles or developing strategies that play to each character's strengths while mitigating their vulnerabilities.

In conclusion, mastering combat strategies in "Metaphor Refantazio" is crucial for overcoming challenges and immersing oneself in the game's rich narrative. Understanding enemy types and their weaknesses, preparing for boss fights, effectively using abilities, and optimizing team composition all contribute to creating a dynamic and engaging combat experience. By employing these strategies, players can navigate the challenges ahead, forging their path through the intricate world of metaphors and transformations.

# Chapter Eight

## Exploration in Metaphor Refantazio

Exploration in Metaphor Refantazio is a rich and immersive experience, inviting players to delve into a beautifully crafted world filled with secrets, diverse environments, and intricate lore. As you embark on your journey, you'll find that exploration is not just a means to an end but a core part of the gameplay that enhances the narrative and deepens your connection to the game's universe.

Key Locations

The world of Metaphor Refantazio is vast, with a variety of key locations that each hold unique stories and challenges. From the bustling markets of the capital city to the serene forests filled with ancient ruins, every area is meticulously designed to draw players in.

In the capital, players can experience the vibrant culture through interactions with NPCs, each of whom has their own tales and quests. The architecture reflects the rich history of the game, with monuments that commemorate great events and figures. As you navigate the streets, look for hidden alleys and rooftops that may lead to secret treasures or lore snippets, providing deeper insights into the game's backstory.

The enchanted forests, on the other hand, offer a stark contrast to the urban landscape. Here, players can explore tranquil glades and dense thickets filled with wildlife. This environment encourages a different pace of exploration, where the sounds of nature serve as both a backdrop and a guide. Many of the forest areas contain puzzles that require keen observation and clever thinking, making the exploration feel rewarding and engaging.

Another notable location is the Forgotten Ruins, a site steeped in mystery and ancient power. This area is not only visually stunning, with crumbling stone structures overrun by nature, but it also serves as a hub for quests and challenges. Players will find that engaging with this environment often leads to encounters with powerful foes and the discovery of rare artifacts.

Secrets and Hidden Areas

One of the most thrilling aspects of exploration in Metaphor Refantazio is the abundance of secrets and hidden areas scattered throughout the world. Developers have cleverly tucked away these elements to reward curious players who take the time to explore off the beaten path.

Look for environmental cues that hint at hidden passages or concealed areas. A slight change in the terrain or an unusual rock formation may indicate a secret entrance. For example, behind a waterfall, players might discover a hidden cave filled with valuable resources or lore tablets that expand on the game's mythology.

Another method to uncover secrets involves utilizing the game's unique Metaphor System. Certain metaphors can reveal hidden paths or activate mechanisms that open up previously inaccessible areas. As you collect and understand these metaphors, you'll find that they not only enhance your character's abilities but also unlock new dimensions of exploration.

Environmental Interactions

The environment in Metaphor Refantazio is designed to be interacted with on multiple levels. Whether it's climbing cliffs, swimming through rivers, or even manipulating elements of the environment through metaphors, players are encouraged to engage deeply with the world around them.

For instance, some locations may feature climbable trees or cliffs that lead to vantage points, allowing you to survey the area and spot secrets below. Waterways can be navigated using boats or swimming, revealing hidden caves or treasures at the riverbed.

Certain puzzles require players to manipulate the environment creatively. This could involve using fire to clear obstacles or growing plants to create paths through dense areas. Engaging with these elements not only fosters a sense of immersion but also reinforces the theme of connection to the world.

Navigating the World

Navigating the world of Metaphor Refantazio can initially seem daunting due to its size and complexity. However, players will quickly find that exploration is facilitated by various tools and systems within the game. A detailed map provides players with key locations and points of interest, while also tracking quests and objectives.

As you progress, unlocking fast travel points becomes essential for efficient exploration. These points are typically located in significant areas and allow you to jump between regions, making it easier to revisit places of interest or tackle quests without excessive backtracking.

Additionally, the game's day-night cycle adds another layer to exploration. Certain events, NPCs, or creatures only appear at specific times, encouraging players to time their explorations strategically. This dynamic environment keeps the gameplay fresh and engaging, as players must adapt their strategies based on the time of day.

Community Interaction and Shared Discoveries

Exploration in Metaphor Refantazio is not just a solitary endeavor. The game encourages players to share their discoveries and experiences, fostering a sense of community. Engaging with other players through forums, social media, or in-game interactions can lead to collaborative exploration efforts.

Community challenges may arise where players work together to uncover a specific secret or defeat a powerful creature guarding a hidden treasure. These shared experiences not only enhance the exploration aspect but also build camaraderie among players, enriching the overall experience of the game.

Conclusion

In Metaphor Refantazio, exploration is an integral component that enhances both the gameplay and narrative. The intricately designed world, filled with diverse locations, secrets, and environmental interactions, invites players to immerse themselves fully in the experience. As you traverse through this captivating universe, remember that every corner holds the potential for discovery, every path may lead to new adventures, and every moment spent exploring is a step deeper into the rich lore and vibrant life of the game. So grab your gear, open your map, and set forth into the wondrous unknown!

# Chapter Nine

## Crafting and Upgrades

Crafting is a vital aspect of Metaphor Refantazio, allowing players to create and enhance gear and items that significantly impact their gameplay experience. Understanding the crafting system can provide a strategic advantage, enabling you to tailor your equipment to suit your playstyle and the challenges you face. Here's an in-depth look at the crafting system, essential items to focus on, and effective strategies for upgrading your equipment.

Crafting in Metaphor Refantazio is designed to empower players by allowing them to create useful items from resources gathered throughout the game world. This system is not just about combining materials; it involves understanding the synergy between components and the benefits they can bring to your character. Players can gather resources from various locations, including the remnants of defeated enemies, flora, and hidden treasure chests. Each material has unique properties, influencing the effectiveness of the items you create. For instance, certain metals may enhance weapon damage, while rare herbs might increase potion potency.

The crafting system also plays a crucial role in the game's economy. Players can trade crafted items, providing an avenue for resource management and interaction with NPCs. This trade system allows players to invest in their crafting skills and focus on creating high-demand items. To craft effectively, you'll need to unlock various recipes, which can be found throughout the world, often tied to quests or hidden in lore. Some recipes are basic, while others require rare components, encouraging exploration and experimentation. Mastering the crafting system can lead to significant advantages in combat and resource management.

When starting your crafting journey, it's essential to focus on specific items that will bolster your capabilities early in the game. Healing potions are crucial for survival, especially during challenging encounters. Crafting healing potions using common herbs can keep you in the fight longer. Upgrading your weapons through crafting not only improves damage output but can also add special effects, such as elemental damage or increased critical hit chances. Prioritize crafting weapons that match your playstyle—whether it's a swift dagger for agility or a heavy axe for brute strength.

Investing in armor upgrades is vital for survivability. Crafting higher-tier armor with reinforced materials can increase your defense and resistance to various damage types. Look for recipes that allow for customizations based on your combat role. Utility items, such as traps, bombs, or tools, can provide advantages in combat or during exploration. Crafting these can turn the tide in difficult battles or help you solve environmental puzzles.

Additionally, create items that temporarily boost your stats, such as increased attack speed or enhanced defense. These can be game-changers during tough boss fights or high-stakes encounters. Crafting bags or containers to increase your inventory space can help manage resources more effectively, allowing you to carry more items without needing to constantly return to town. Don't overlook the significance of Metaphor Crystals, unique items that enable you to harness the power of the metaphor system, amplifying your abilities and allowing for more profound interactions within the game's narrative. Gather rare materials to craft these crystals and enhance your metaphor usage.

As you progress through Metaphor Refantazio, upgrading your equipment becomes increasingly important to remain competitive against tougher enemies and challenges. It's essential to prioritize high-value items by identifying the equipment that has served you well or offers the most potential for improvement. Focus your resources on upgrading these key items rather than spreading your materials too thin across multiple pieces.

Gathering rare materials is crucial for upgrades, as certain enhancements require components that may not be readily available. Make a concerted effort to explore hidden areas or defeat powerful enemies to obtain these materials. You can also trade with NPCs to acquire hard-to-find items. When upgrading, consider the synergy between different components. Some materials may provide bonuses when combined with specific items, leading to more powerful upgrades. Experiment with different combinations to discover the most effective enhancements.

Regularly check for new recipes that become available as you progress in the game. Some upgrades may only be unlocked through specific quests or achievements, so stay vigilant in seeking out these opportunities. Track your inventory and manage your resources carefully. Avoid hoarding items that could be used for upgrades, and regularly evaluate what you have to prioritize materials for equipment that will enhance your current playstyle.

Once you've completed an upgrade, test the new gear in various combat scenarios. Pay attention to how the changes impact your performance. This will help you understand which upgrades are most effective and guide future enhancements. Engaging with the player community can also provide valuable insights regarding crafting and upgrades. Online forums, social media, and dedicated Discord servers can offer tips and strategies for the best approaches to take.

By incorporating these strategies into your gameplay, you can ensure that your character remains equipped to handle any challenges that arise in Metaphor Refantazio. Crafting and upgrading are not just supplemental activities; they are integral to mastering the game and fully enjoying the rich experience it offers. Remember, the journey is as important as the destination, so take the time to explore, experiment, and engage with every aspect of crafting and upgrades in this captivating world.

# Chapter Ten

## Endgame Content

Once you've completed the main story of Metaphor Refantazio, the journey is far from over. The endgame content offers a wealth of activities and challenges that encourage exploration, skill mastery, and community engagement. This phase of the game is designed to keep players invested, providing opportunities to test your abilities, uncover hidden secrets, and connect with fellow players.

Post-story activities present a chance to delve deeper into the game's rich lore and explore areas that may have been inaccessible during the main narrative. After the conclusion of the primary storyline, players can embark on new quests that expand on character arcs, resolve lingering plot threads, or introduce entirely new challenges. These quests often feature tougher enemies and more complex puzzles, encouraging you to revisit locations with fresh eyes and strategies.

One significant aspect of post-story content is the chance to uncover hidden collectibles and lore items that enhance your understanding of the game world. Many of these items provide insights into the history of the factions you encountered, the mythology surrounding the game's universe, or character backstories that were hinted at throughout the main story. Engaging with this content not only enriches your experience but also gives you a sense of closure as you learn more about the world you've been navigating.

In addition to new quests, players can participate in a variety of side activities that may include crafting and resource gathering, exploration challenges, or even mini-games that test your skills in unique ways. These activities often yield valuable rewards, such as rare crafting materials or powerful gear that can help you tackle the tougher content that awaits.

For players seeking a higher level of challenge, high-level content is abundant in the endgame. This includes elite quests and dungeons that are specifically designed for seasoned players who have mastered the game's mechanics. These challenges often feature powerful bosses with unique abilities and attack patterns, requiring you to strategize and cooperate with other players or optimize your character's build to succeed.

High-level dungeons often include mechanics that push your understanding of the game to its limits. You might face timed challenges that require quick thinking and agile reactions or encounter enemies that necessitate precise coordination with teammates. Engaging in these challenges not only tests your skills but also rewards you with exclusive loot, including unique weapons, armor sets, and rare crafting materials that can only be obtained through these rigorous encounters.

Another exciting feature of the endgame is the introduction of seasonal events and community challenges. These events often coincide with real-world holidays or in-game celebrations, providing fresh content and limited-time rewards. Players can participate in unique quests, compete in leaderboards, or collaborate to achieve community goals, fostering a sense of camaraderie among players. These events often offer exclusive items that can't be obtained elsewhere, making participation even more enticing.

Community events also serve as a great way to connect with other players. The shared experience of tackling challenges or completing objectives together creates a lively atmosphere where players can share tips, strategies, and their excitement for the game. Many players find joy in these interactions, forming friendships and alliances that extend beyond the game itself.

Additionally, the game developers frequently engage with the community during these events, providing updates and introducing new features based on player feedback. This continuous cycle of interaction keeps the game fresh and ensures that the community feels valued and heard.

As you dive into the endgame content of Metaphor Refantazio, remember that exploration is key. The world is rich with secrets, and the challenges you face are designed to encourage you to push your limits. Whether you're revisiting familiar locations with new objectives, facing off against formidable foes in high-level content, or engaging with the community during seasonal events, there's no shortage of activities to keep you entertained.

Ultimately, the endgame content of Metaphor Refantazio is about more than just completing challenges; it's about deepening your connection to the game world and the community surrounding it. So gear up, gather your friends, and prepare for a wealth of experiences that await you beyond the main story. Your adventure is just beginning, and the possibilities are endless.

www.ingramcontent.com/pod-product-compliance
Lightning Source LLC
LaVergne TN
LVHW051713050326
832903LV00032B/4185